THIS JOURNAL BELONGS TO

The Ultimate Friendship Journal: An Interactive Guide to
Making New Friends & Treasuring the Ones You've Got
Copyright © 2025 Girl Scouts of the United States of America
All rights reserved. Manufactured in Johor, Malaysia.
No part of this book may be used or reproduced in any manner whatsoever without written
permission except in the case of brief quotations embodied in critical articles and reviews.
For information address HarperCollins Children's Books, a division of HarperCollins Publishers,
195 Broadway, New York, NY 10007.
www.harpercollinschildrens.com

ISBN 978-0-06-331787-1

The artist used Photoshop to create the digital illustrations for this book.
Typography by Stephanie Hays
24 25 26 27 28   COS   10 9 8 7 6 5 4 3 2 1
First Edition

girl scouts

THE ULTIMATE FRIENDSHIP JOURNAL

ILLUSTRATED BY BRENNA VAUGHAN

HARPER
An Imprint of HarperCollinsPublishers

INTRODUCTION

FRIENDS ARE ONE OF THE BEST THINGS ABOUT LIFE, PERIOD.

There's nothing better than spending time with a friend (or two or more). You laugh with your friends. You cry with your friends. And you do almost everything in between with your friends, like practicing that really hard dance routine, studying for a math test, or working together to cheer up another friend when they're sad.

Our friends help us be our best selves, and we do the same for them. A friend can support you through a tough time, open your eyes to seeing the world in a new way, or inspire you to try something you never thought you'd be into.

But friendship—making friends, keeping friends, being a great friend—isn't always easy. You may be wondering . . .

- ♥ HOW CAN I MAKE NEW FRIENDS, ESPECIALLY IF I FEEL SHY OR AM IN A NEW PLACE?
- ♥ CAN MY FRIEND AND I EVER BE FRIENDS AGAIN AFTER A FIGHT?
- ♥ HOW DO I KEEP A LONG-DISTANCE FRIENDSHIP STRONG?
- ♥ HOW CAN I BE THERE FOR A FRIEND WHO'S FEELING REALLY DOWN?
- ♥ WHAT DO I DO IF I DON'T LIKE THE SAME THINGS MY FRIENDS LIKE?
- ♥ HOW DO I BALANCE FRIENDSHIP WITH RESPONSIBILITIES, LIKE CHORES AND SCHOOL?
- ♥ HOW CAN I MAKE SURE MY FRIENDS KNOW HOW MUCH I APPRECIATE THEM?
- ♥ AND PROBABLY LOTS OF OTHER THINGS.

Let this book be your guide—your ultimate friendship guide. In these pages, you'll find quizzes, drawing and writing activities, inspirational quotes, and more, all designed to help you through the best and bumpiest parts of friendship.

READY? HERE WE GO!

"WE ALL WANT TO FIND SOMEBODY TO SEE OUR SIGHTS WITH AND HEAR THINGS WITH AND EXPERIENCE THINGS WITH."

—TAYLOR SWIFT

MAKING FRIENDS CAN BE EXCITING,

but sometimes it's not as simple as it sounds. You might feel shy, scared, or unsure if a new friend will like you for who you are. You might have no idea what to say to a new person to break the ice.

Here's the thing: if you can work your way through those feelings and worries, what waits on the other side is a potential new friend.

And that excited spark you feel when you bond with someone who might just become a friend for life? There's nothing better.

One of the most important things to do when you want to make a new friend is to put yourself out there. Taking that first step to break the ice is a *big* step, so if this feels overwhelming or makes you nervous, that's OK.

ARE YOU PUTTING YOURSELF OUT THERE TO MAKE NEW FRIENDS? TAKE THIS QUIZ TO FIND OUT.

1. YOU'RE OUT RUNNING ERRANDS WITH YOUR FAMILY AND YOU SEE SOMEONE AROUND YOUR AGE WHO IS WEARING THE EXACT SAME PAIR OF SNEAKERS AS YOU—WHICH JUST HAPPENS TO BE YOUR FAVORITE PAIR. WHAT DO YOU DO NEXT?

    A. Introduce yourself and point out that you're sneaker twins.
    B. Catch their eye and smile, hoping they'll approach you.
    C. Keep your eyes trained on your own sneaks until it's time to go.

2. YOU DON'T KNOW ANY OF THE OTHER KIDS AT YOUR COUSIN'S BIRTHDAY PARTY. WHO DO YOU HANG OUT WITH?

    A. You say hi to the nearest group of kids and hope they'll be friendly.
    B. You glue yourself to your cousin's side for the whole party.
    C. Forget the kids—you're hanging out with your cousin's dog, who already knows and loves you.

3. DURING A GROUP PROJECT FOR SCHOOL, YOU AND YOUR GROUP MATES REALLY BONDED. WHAT DO YOU DO NOW THAT THE PROJECT IS OVER?

    A. Seek them out in class and try to get a recess hang going.
    B. Keep the group chat buzzing but never ask if you can meet up after school.
    C. Let the bond fizzle because you don't know how to tell them you want to be friends outside of the project.

4. YOU REALLY LOVE MATH AND SCIENCE, AND YOU'VE ALSO ALWAYS WANTED TO JOIN THE ART CLUB. YOU DON'T KNOW ANYONE ELSE IN THE CLUB, THOUGH. WHAT DO YOU DO WHEN THE NEW SCHOOL YEAR STARTS?

    A. Sign up for the art club right away. It's time to pursue your passion.
    B. Joke to your math/science friends about joining the art club but don't actually do it.
    C. Stick with what you're good at and keep your interest in art a secret for another year.

5. THERE'S A NEW KID AT SCHOOL, AND YOU SEE THEM SITTING ALONE AT LUNCHTIME. WHAT DO YOU DO?

A. Get up from your table and go sit with them.
B. Wave hi and give a friendly smile but stay where you are.
C. Pretend you don't see them. They'll make plenty of friends on their own.

RESULTS

MOSTLY A: You're very friendly and outgoing and take every opportunity to make a new friend. Make sure to remember that others might be shyer than you are, and so it could take them a little longer to warm up to you—be patient and keep being kind!

MOSTLY B: You put yourself in situations where you could make new friends, but you hang back a little. Try to challenge yourself to put yourself out there a little more. Try introducing yourself to someone new or suggest getting together with someone you haven't hung out with before outside of school. Take more initiative and you may find a new friend!

MOSTLY C: You could put yourself out there more to make new friends. It can feel hard, but it's worth it. You don't even have to start with a complete stranger: try saying hi to someone at school who you've known for a long time but never really talked to. Start small and ask how their weekend was, then build up to asking if they want to pair up in gym class for an activity. Keep trying and you may make a new friend!

PART OF MAKING NEW FRIENDS is deciding who you want to be friends with. What are the qualities you look for in a friend? Do you want to be friends with someone who gets your jokes? Someone who listens? Someone who shares your love of animals?

COMPLETE THIS SENTENCE WITH THE QUALITIES THAT DESCRIBE YOUR POTENTIAL NEW FRIEND.

I want to be friends with someone who . . .

ON THE FLIP SIDE, what are the qualities that *you* want a new friend to see in you? Are you known for your loyalty? Your generosity? Are you really good at geography and willing to help a buddy study?

COMPLETE THE SENTENCE WITH THE QUALITIES THAT DESCRIBE WHAT KIND OF FRIEND YOU ARE.

I want my new friend to see that I am . . .

▸ _____
▸ _____
▸ _____
▸ _____
▸ _____
▸ _____
▸ _____
▸ _____
▸ _____
▸ _____
▸ _____
▸ _____
▸ _____
▸ _____

MAKING A NEW FRIEND is a little bit like building an ice cream sundae: you're creating something from different ingredients, hoping and working to find the perfect combination (of friends).

You may try two scoops of shared interests, a sprinkle of independence, and a drizzle of the same sense of humor. Or any combination you think would be best! What ingredients do you think would make a really great forever friendship?

And while we're on the subject, if you're looking for something to do with a new friend, here's a recipe for a tasty ice cream sundae (the kind you eat, not the friendship kind) that you could make together:

Recipe

- ♥ Three scoops of ice cream, possibly each a different flavor (dairy-free if you prefer)
- ♥ A drizzle of your choice of syrup (caramel, chocolate, toffee, or all three)
- ♥ A dash of sprinkles
- ♥ Half a banana, sliced up
- ♥ A dollop of whipped cream
- ♥ Not one but two cherries on top
- ♥ Don't forget the spoons!

THINK ABOUT all the pairs and groups of friends you see around you, every day. This includes pairs or groups of friends at your school, the dogs you see playing together at the dog park, celebrity besties, and duos, trios, or groups from TV, movies, and books. . . . List them here (examples: Beyoncé and Kelly Rowland, your sibling and their best friend since kindergarten, Kristoff and Sven from *Frozen*):

BEST FRIENDS

WHAT ARE THESE FRIENDSHIPS LIKE?

HOW ARE THESE FRIENDS GOOD FRIENDS TO EACH OTHER?

WHAT CAN YOU LEARN FROM THE FRIENDSHIPS YOU SEE AROUND YOU?

WHAT DO YOU ADMIRE ABOUT THESE FRIENDSHIPS?

FRIENDSHIP CAN BLOSSOM ANYWHERE!

You can make friends from all the different parts of your life. You could have a ton in common with some people, while others you see only at sports practice or debate club.

It's pretty cool to think that different friends bring out different parts of you. You probably do the same for them.

Fill out this flower to represent all the spaces and places where you have and could make friends. (Hint: You are in the center, and each petal is a different part of your social life and the friends you have there.)

Some examples are: in the cafeteria, during recess, at sports practice, at Girl Scouts, the library—anywhere you spend time.

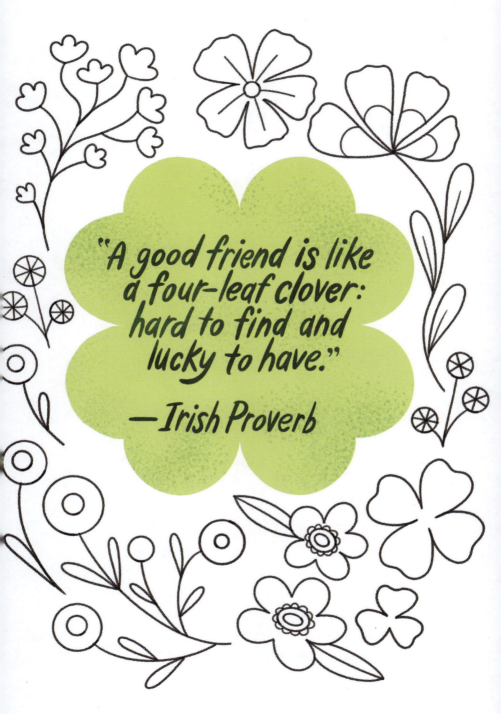

ONE OF THE FIRST THINGS you need to do when you're approaching a potential new friend is . . . say something! It can be hard to think of what to say, though, especially if you're feeling shy. But you can start by introducing yourself.

Fill in the blanks in these speech bubbles to give you some ideas for what you can say the next time you need to start a new convo.

Hi! My name is
_____.
What's yours?

Did you see
the latest
_____ movie?

You're really good at _____.
Can you help me with my
_____?

I really like your
_____.

Who's your
favorite
_____?

Did you write down the _____
homework assignment?

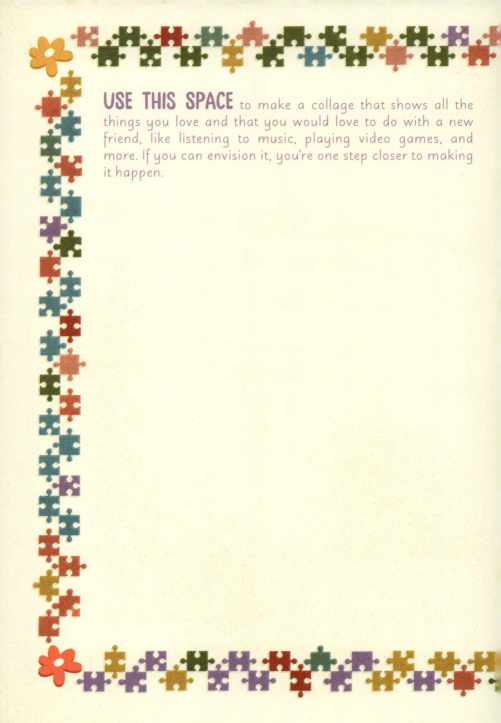

USE THIS SPACE to make a collage that shows all the things you love and that you would love to do with a new friend, like listening to music, playing video games, and more. If you can envision it, you're one step closer to making it happen.

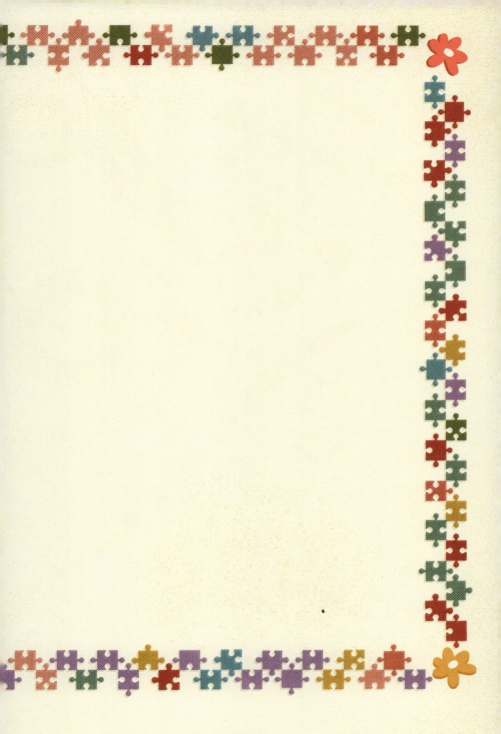

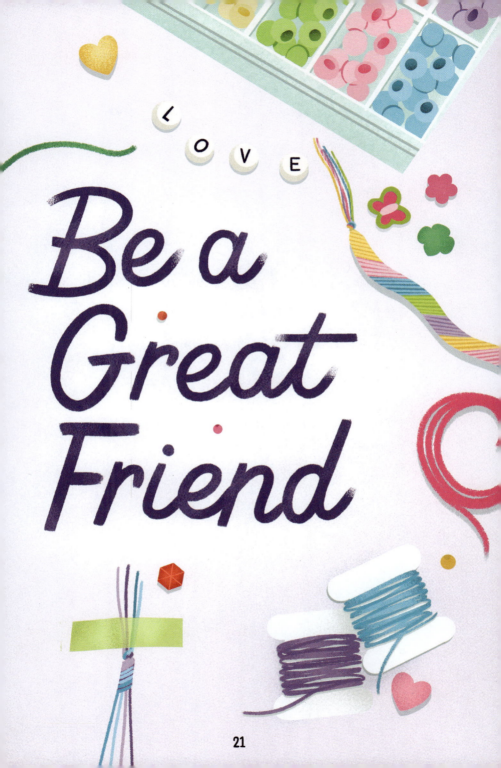

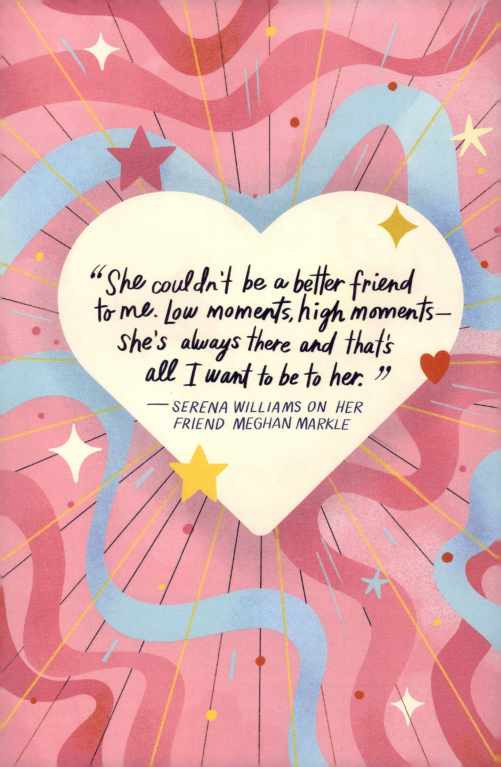

ONCE YOU'VE MADE A FRIEND (OR MORE THAN ONE),

the next step is to be a good friend, again and again. But how can you be the *best* friend you can be?

It's normal to wonder . . .

- ♥ WHAT MAKES SOMEONE A GOOD FRIEND?
- ♥ HOW CAN YOU BE THERE FOR A FRIEND IN NEED?
- ♥ WHAT CAN YOU LEARN FROM OTHER FRIENDSHIPS YOU SEE?
- ♥ AND MORE . . .

Being a good friend will bring lots of joy to you and to your friend(s). It's worth giving it your best try!

QUIZ

PART OF BEING A GREAT FRIEND IS BEING PRESENT, EVEN IF YOU'RE PHYSICALLY FAR AWAY. ARE YOU THERE FOR YOUR FRIENDS? TAKE THIS QUIZ TO FIND OUT.

1. YOUR FRIEND'S FAMILY IS MOVING TO ANOTHER STATE. WHAT DO YOU DO WHEN THEY BREAK THE NEWS?

A. Cry, cry, cry, and ask your friend if they have a tissue.
B. Give your friend a giant hug and promise you'll keep in touch.
C. Start begging your family to move, too, so your friend won't be alone at their new school.

2. YOUR FRIEND HASN'T BEEN ANSWERING YOUR MESSAGES AND SEEMS DISTANT AT SCHOOL. WHAT DO YOU DO?

A. Corner them and demand to know why they're mad at you.
B. Send one more message telling them you're there to listen if they want to talk, then give them some space to come to you when they're ready.
C. Write them a long note telling them you'll do *anything* to be their friend again.

3. YOUR FRIEND'S GRANDPARENT PASSED AWAY, AND YOUR FRIEND IS COMING BACK TO SCHOOL AFTER A WEEK OF GRIEVING WITH THEIR FAMILY. WHAT DO YOU DO WHEN YOU SEE THEM?

A. Tell them about your latest fight with your sibling. Your sister can be so rude sometimes.
B. Remind them that you're there for them and that you'll follow their lead—if they want to talk about their grandparent, you'll listen, and if they don't, you're happy to tell them about the past week at school.
C. Give them the batch of their favorite cookies you stayed up late baking. So what if you're tired? Your friend *loves* these cookies.

4. YOUR FRIEND TELLS YOU ABOUT THEIR CRUSH AND ASKS YOU TO KEEP IT A SECRET. WHAT DO YOU DO?

A. Tell your friend a secret of your own to make things even.
B. Your lips are zipped unless your friend tells you otherwise.
C. Stay up late coming up with an elaborate plan to get your friend and their crush to sit next to each other at lunch.

RESULTS

MOSTLY A: Sometimes you're a little too focused on *you* to be there for your friends as much as they might need you. Try this: next time your friend is sad and comes to you, pause for a moment and think about what you would want them to do if you were sad. Then do that for them.

MOSTLY B: You're very supportive without smothering your friend—nice job finding that balance. Just make sure your friends are there for you when you need their support, too.

MOSTLY C: You tend to get so caught up in being there for your friends that you forget to be there for yourself. Schedule some "me time" into your weekend to reconnect with your own needs.

✻ LET'S BRAINSTORM WAYS TO BE A GOOD FRIEND. ✻

CAN YOU LIST FIFTY? HERE ARE A FEW TO GET YOU STARTED:

1. Help your friend with their math homework when they're having trouble.
2. Plan a surprise birthday party for your friend.
3. Support your friend while they practice for the school musical auditions.
4.
5.
6.
7.
8.
9.
10.
11.
12.
13.
14.
15.
16.
17.
18.
19.
20.
21.
22.
23.
24.

25.
26.
27.
28.
29.
30.
31.
32.
33.
34.
35.
36.
37.
38.
39.
40.
41.
42.
43.
44.
45.
46.
47.
48.
49.
50.

BEING THERE FOR YOUR FRIENDS can sometimes mean helping out when they ask for help. And the same goes for your friend(s) helping you when you need it.

HELP NEEDED

Can you think of some times that you needed—or might need in the future—help from a friend? For example:

- ♥ YOU'RE HAVING A HARD TIME UNDERSTANDING THE LATEST UNIT IN SCIENCE CLASS.
- ♥ YOU'RE FIGHTING WITH YOUR SISTER, AND IT'S MAKING YOU FEEL SAD AND ANGRY.
- ♥ YOU WANT TO JOIN THE BASKETBALL TEAM AND NEED SOMEONE TO PRACTICE WITH TO IMPROVE YOUR SKILLS.

_____
_____
_____
_____
_____
_____
_____
_____
_____
_____
_____
_____
_____
_____
_____
_____

YOU GOT THIS.

It can be tough to ask for help. How would you ask for help in those situations? What would be the best way a friend could help you? For example:

- ♥ CAN YOU HELP ME STUDY FOR THE NEXT SCIENCE QUIZ? WE CAN MAKE FLASH CARDS TOGETHER OR ASK EACH OTHER QUESTIONS.
- ♥ I'M FIGHTING WITH MY SISTER, CAN YOU LISTEN FOR A LITTLE BIT WHILE I GET MY FEELINGS OUT?
- ♥ WILL YOU PRACTICE DRIBBLING SKILLS WITH ME AFTER SCHOOL?

? _____

? _____

? _____

? _____

? _____

? _____

? _____

WHAT MAKES A FRIEND GREAT?

Circle all the words from the list below that you think describe a great friend. Write in any other descriptions you would use.

Smart

Asks lots of questions

Funny

Honest

Outgoing

Generous

Thoughtful

Loves pizza

chatty

Shy

athletic

creative

Sensitive

Likes all the things you like

A good listener

PICK ONE OF THE "GREAT FRIEND" DESCRIPTIONS FROM THE PREVIOUS PAGE AND WRITE ABOUT A TIME IT DESCRIBED YOU PERFECTLY.

For example, was there a time your creativity was important in one of your friendships? Or maybe your love of pizza made you a really great friend one afternoon when your friend was craving that cheesy goodness.

DIFFERENT PEOPLE express their feelings in different ways. You might show a friend that you appreciate their friendship by giving them a gift. They might prefer to use words to show you they care. And you both might change it up now and then and show how much the friendship means to you by giving each other a high five.

REMEMBER: you want your ways of showing appreciation to be wanted and appreciated, just like you would want your friend to show you appreciation in a way you're cool with. Always ask a friend if they'd like how you plan to show appreciation before actually doing anything. For example: "I know how much you love music. Would you like me to make you a playlist?" or "I really love baking. Would you like to try one of my creations?" That way, you can learn what makes your friend feel appreciated and you don't make your friend feel uncomfortable. Don't be upset if your friend says no—everyone likes different things.

HOW CAN YOU SHOW YOUR FRIENDS THAT YOU APPRECIATE THEIR FRIENDSHIP? CIRCLE ALL THAT APPLY.

- Baking them a yummy treat
- Sending them a cute animal photo
- Saying I appreciate you
- Creating your own secret handshake
- Making them a friendship bracelet
- Building them a happy music playlist
- Helping them do their chores while you're at their home
- Spending one whole day together every weekend
- Cheering them on at their big game
- Telling them they are a great friend

WHAT ARE SOME OTHERS? LIST THEM HERE

-
-
-
-
-
-
-
-
-
-

NOTHING SAYS "FRIENDSHIP" to the world like a bold, bright friendship bracelet. Design a friendship bracelet here for you and your friend(s):

NEED SOME INSPIRATION?

- BLUE COULD SYMBOLIZE LOYALTY.
- PURPLE COULD SYMBOLIZE FRIENDSHIP.
- RED COULD SYMBOLIZE GOOD LUCK.
- YELLOW COULD SYMBOLIZE FRIENDLINESS.
- ORANGE COULD SYMBOLIZE HAPPINESS.
- GREEN COULD SYMBOLIZE HOPE.

Of course, your design is totally up to you. You can decide what the colors in your bracelets mean. Maybe certain colors mean something special to you and your friends for your own reasons!

NEVER MADE A BRAIDED FRIENDSHIP BRACELET?

Here's how to make a spiral staircase bracelet:

1. Choose three to eight colors (the more you choose, the thicker your bracelet will be) of embroidery thread. Cut the strings to equal length—measure from your shoulder to your fingertip to make sure you have enough—and tie them into a knot at one end. Tape the knotted end to the surface you're working on to keep it in place as you work.

2. To make a "forward knot": Take one string, pull it slightly to the left, and fold it over the other strings. If it helps to visualize this, imagine you are making the number 4 with your strings.

3. Tuck the end of that string under and through the fold you made. Pull the end of the string tight.

4. Repeat the forward knot steps four more times with that same string. Then do a forward knot five times with the second string, then the third string, and so on with as many strings as you've included in your bracelet.

5. When you've reached the length you want your bracelet to be, tie the two ends together and cut off any remaining loose string.

ACTIVE LISTENING is a way of listening and then responding that shows you really get what's being said to you. This is an important skill for a good friend to have, especially if one of your friends wants to talk to you about a problem. Here are some tips for active listening:

♥ Don't feel you have to fix the problem. Sometimes just listening is enough.
♥ Only respond once your friend has said what they need to say and has stopped talking—don't interrupt!
♥ Use encouraging body language like nodding and making eye contact to show you are listening and interested.
♥ Ask questions.

THINKING ABOUT THESE TIPS, ARE YOU AN ACTIVE LISTENER? HOW COULD YOU IMPROVE AS AN ACTIVE LISTENER?

_____
_____
_____
_____
_____
_____
_____

TRY THIS:

Listen to a friend talk for two minutes. Don't interrupt. When the two minutes are up, tell them what you heard them say. Then switch and repeat.

A GOOD FRIEND IS THERE FOR THEIR FRIEND(S) WHEN THEY NEED A LITTLE HELP.

WHAT ARE THREE WAYS YOU'VE RECENTLY HELPED A FRIEND?

If you aren't sure how to help, ask your friend(s) what they need. Put yourself in their shoes and think about what *you* might need from your friends if you were going through the same thing.

-
-
-

HOW CAN YOU HELP A FRIEND WHO NEEDS IT RIGHT NOW?

YOU OBVIOUSLY WANT TO BE A GOOD FRIEND

and support and help your friends when they need it. But you don't want to lose yourself in their problems.

What are some ways you can do something for yourself while also helping a friend through a challenge? Read through the following examples and then add some ideas of your own.

♥ WHEN YOU RETURN HOME FROM COMFORTING A FRIEND WHO IS GRIEVING A FAMILY MEMBER, TAKE SOME QUIET TIME TO YOURSELF AND TAKE FIVE CALMING BREATHS TO HELP PROCESS THE HEAVY SITUATION. BREATHE IN FOR FIVE SECONDS, BREATHE OUT FOR FIVE SECONDS—AND REPEAT FIVE TIMES.

♥ KEEP A GRATITUDE JOURNAL. EVERY NIGHT BEFORE BED, WRITE DOWN THREE THINGS YOU'RE GRATEFUL FOR IN YOUR OWN LIFE. THIS WILL KEEP YOU FOCUSED ON SOME OF THE GOOD THINGS IN LIFE, NO MATTER WHAT CHALLENGES YOU OR YOUR FRIENDS ARE FACING.

"*If you have three people in your life that you can trust, you can consider yourself the luckiest person in the whole world.*"

—Selena Gomez

IT CAN FEEL NICE when a friend confides a problem to you. It means they trust you and value your support. And you want to be a good friend and keep their troubles to yourself, right? But some secrets shouldn't be kept.

It's hard to tell an adult your friend's secret, but sometimes it's the right thing to do. If your friend is in danger, someone is hurting them, they're hurting someone else, or they're hurting themselves, it's time to tell an adult. Pick an adult who you trust, who—even if they might be disappointed in your or your friend's behavior—will definitely have your backs. An adult who will want to help instead of just getting mad. An adult who you think will know what to do next.

WHO ARE THE ADULTS YOU TRUST TO HELP YOU AND YOUR FRIEND? MAKE A LIST HERE SO YOU CAN COME BACK TO IT IF YOU EVER NEED TO:

P.S. There are more resources for adult help at the end of this journal—just flip to page 139 if you need it.

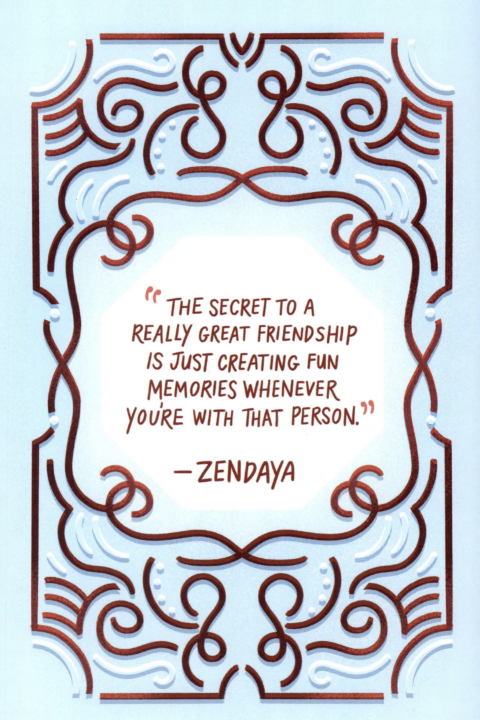

IF YOU COULD AWARD YOURSELF a friendship medal, what would it be for? (Example: Best at Making Friendship Bracelets medal)

DRAW THE MEDAL HERE:

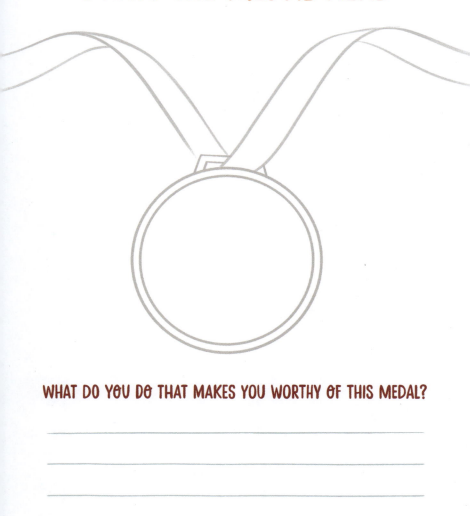

WHAT DO YOU DO THAT MAKES YOU WORTHY OF THIS MEDAL?

_____
_____
_____
_____

NOW THAT YOU'VE THOUGHT MORE about what kind of friend you are now, it's time to think about how you'd like to grow as a friend moving forward.

What are your friendship goals for the next year?

Here are a few examples to get you started:

- ♥ I WANT TO SHARE A FAMILY TRADITION WITH A FRIEND WHO I THINK WILL ENJOY IT.
- ♥ I WANT TO PARTICIPATE IN MY FIRST SLEEPOVER AWAY FROM HOME.
- ♥ I WANT TO IMPROVE MY ACTIVE-LISTENING SKILLS SO I CAN BE THERE FOR A FRIEND WHO NEEDS TO TALK.

FRIENDSHIP GOALS

- _____
  _____
- _____
  _____
  _____
- _____
  _____
- _____
  _____
  _____

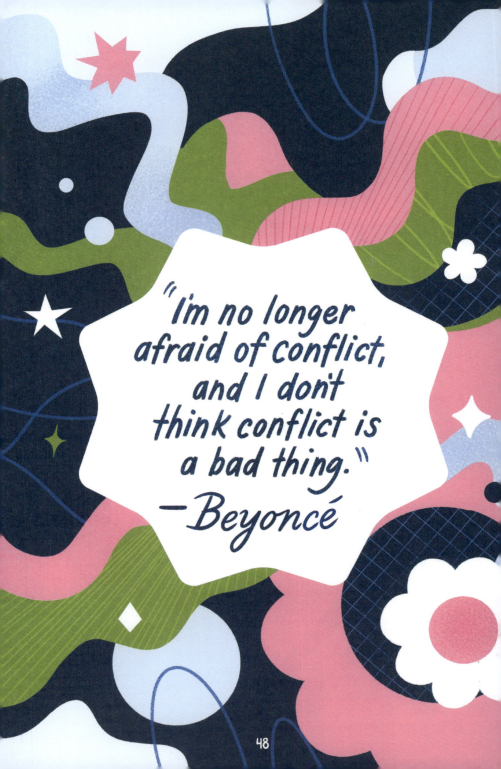

YOU AND YOUR FRIEND(S) COULD BE FRIENDS FOREVER

and ever and ever, and guess what? Conflict is still going to come up between you. It's totally normal and even healthy for a friendship to have ups and downs.

How can you handle conflict when it happens?

- ♥ CAN YOU STAY FRIENDS AFTER A FIGHT?
- ♥ HOW DO YOU COMPROMISE?
- ♥ WHAT DO YOU DO WHEN YOU FEEL EXCLUDED BY YOUR FRIENDS?
- ♥ CAN YOU STAY CLOSE WITH A FRIEND WHO MOVES FAR AWAY?

Don't worry, it's possible to get through conflict in a friendship. Hopefully your friendship will come out stronger on the other side.

FIRST THINGS FIRST: HOW HEALTHY IS YOUR FRIENDSHIP? TAKE THIS QUIZ TO FIND OUT.

1. WHICH SNACK COMBO ARE YOU AND YOUR FRIEND MOST LIKE?
- **A.** Peanut butter and jelly.
- **B.** Pickles and ice cream.
- **C.** Popcorn and M&M'S.

2. YOUR FAMILY OFTEN SAYS YOU AND YOUR FRIEND ARE . . .
- **A.** Twinning.
- **B.** Frenemies.
- **C.** Friends.

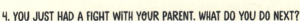

3. OVER THE WEEKEND, YOU AND YOUR FRIEND ARE MOST LIKELY TO BE FOUND . . .
- **A.** Hanging out all day and having a sleepover at night.
- **B.** In a fight.
- **C.** Sometimes hanging out together, sometimes doing your own things.

4. YOU JUST HAD A FIGHT WITH YOUR PARENT. WHAT DO YOU DO NEXT?
- **A.** Video chat with your friend to vent about the fight for hours.
- **B.** Write in your journal, the only friend you trust.
- **C.** Message your friend about it, but don't get into the details.

5. YOU WANT TO JOIN THE SOCCER TEAM. YOUR FRIEND WANTS TO DO VOLLEYBALL. WHAT DO YOU DO?
- **A.** You both try out for both teams and do whichever one you both make.
- **B.** Yell at each other because you never want to do the same things.
- **C.** Try out for your own teams and make plans to cheer each other on at games.

RESULTS

MOSTLY A: Your friendship is as close as can be. You and your friend might want to build some separate time into your friendship, just to make sure you have time for yourself, other people, and hobbies.

MOSTLY B: It might be time for a friendship break. Take some time apart and see if you miss each other enough to come back and rebuild your friendship.

MOSTLY C: Your friendship is very healthy. Maybe you're besties, maybe you're not—even best friends have different interests and spend time apart. If you do want to spend more time with your friend, try inviting them over for dinner with your family, or suggesting you do an after-school activity together.

"ANYTHING IS POSSIBLE WHEN YOU HAVE THE RIGHT PEOPLE THERE TO SUPPORT YOU."

— Misty Copeland

WHEN A FRIENDSHIP GETS TOUGH, whatever the reason, you might want some advice from someone *outside* the friendship to help you get through it. Someone you trust, who is a good listener—and maybe someone who has been through friendship tough times of their own.

Who in your life can you go to for advice about friendship issues? Make a list here.

WHO TO TALK TO:

good advice

USE THIS SPACE TO WRITE DOWN THE ADVICE FROM THE PEOPLE ON THE PREVIOUS PAGE. THAT WAY YOU'LL BE ABLE TO RETURN TO IT WHEN YOU NEED IT.

THINK BACK to a fight you had with a friend. How did it make you feel? Circle all that apply:

Scared

Angry

Energized

Tired

Anxious

Frustrated

Sad

Silly

Are there other words to describe how the fight made you feel that aren't listed above?

_____
_____
_____

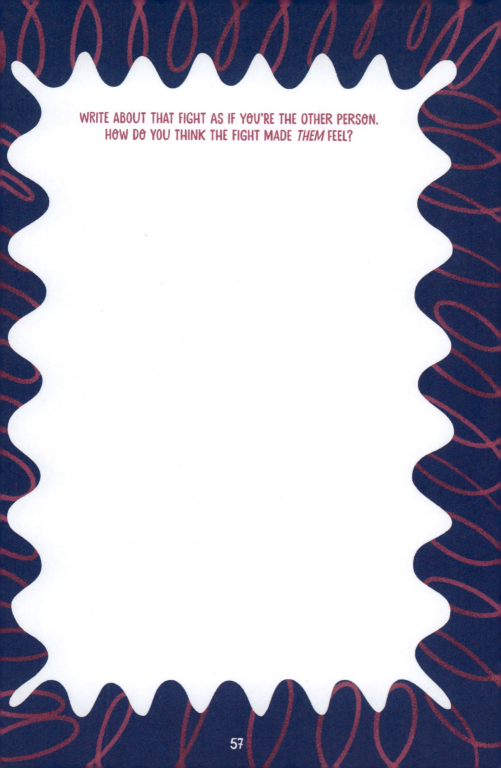
WRITE ABOUT THAT FIGHT AS IF YOU'RE THE OTHER PERSON. HOW DO YOU THINK THE FIGHT MADE *THEM* FEEL?

IS THERE ANYTHING YOU THINK YOU COULD HAVE DONE DIFFERENTLY IN THE FIGHT, NOW THAT YOU'VE THOUGHT ABOUT THE OTHER PERSON'S SIDE OF IT?

WHAT HAPPENS when a friend hurts your feelings? Or does something that you think is wrong? What do you do next when . . .

- ♥ YOUR FRIEND EXCLUDES A CLASSMATE WHILE PLAYING A GAME AT RECESS?
- ♥ YOUR FRIEND SAYS SOMETHING UNKIND ABOUT YOUR OUTFIT?
- ♥ YOUR FRIEND ASKS TO COPY YOUR HOMEWORK BECAUSE THEY DIDN'T DO THEIRS?
- ♥ OR YOUR FRIEND DOES SOMETHING ELSE THAT DOESN'T FEEL RIGHT TO YOU?

One way to handle these situations is to talk to your friend about what they did and how it made you feel. A great way to start a conversation like that is to use "I" statements.

"I" statements focus on how *you* felt about the action/behavior, rather than what *someone else* did/said or didn't do/say. Using an "I" statement allows you to let your feelings out without attacking or blaming your friend in a way that might hurt *their* feelings. An "I" statement is specific and focuses on how a friend's behavior affected *you*.

HERE ARE SOME "I" STATEMENT EXAMPLES:

I FELT EMBARRASSED AND INSULTED WHEN YOU MADE FUN OF MY NEW SHOES IN FRONT OF EVERYONE. IF YOU DON'T LIKE SOMETHING I'M WEARING, CAN YOU TELL ME IN PRIVATE INSTEAD OF MOCKING ME IN FRONT OF OTHER PEOPLE?

WHEN YOU INCLUDED ME IN TAG AT RECESS BUT EXCLUDED SARAH, I FELT ANXIOUS BECAUSE I'M NOT COMFORTABLE EXCLUDING OTHERS WHEN THERE'S ROOM FOR EVERYONE. CAN WE TALK ABOUT HOW TO INCLUDE EVERYONE IN OUR GAMES?

NOW COME UP WITH A FEW OF YOUR OWN:

"If they're willing to say
I think you could do
better, it means they're
going to bat for you."

— Olivia Rodrigo

LET'S SUPPORT EACH OTHER

There are different types of feedback you might want to give a friend—one type is letting a friend know they hurt you, like the examples on the previous page. But you also might want to give your friend feedback to help them be the best them they can be.

Being a supportive friend doesn't always mean total agreement. When given thoughtfully and sensitively, honest feedback can be a great act of friendship.

Feedback can be positive (*You came up with so many good ideas for our class fundraiser!*) or constructive (*I noticed you were really nervous during your class presentation today. How do you feel it went? Next time, we can practice together beforehand and maybe you won't feel as nervous.*).

TRY THIS:

Offer a suggestion with your feedback to make it more constructive. Here is an example and fill-in-the-blank prompt to help you practice giving honest—but not hurtful—feedback to a friend:

> DURING OUR GROUP PROJECT MEETING, I NOTICED THAT YOU TOOK CHARGE AND ASSIGNED EVERYONE A ROLE IN THE PROJECT. IT MADE ME FEEL LIKE I DIDN'T HAVE A SAY IN THE PROJECT. NEXT TIME, YOU COULD TRY ASKING EVERYONE TO WEIGH IN WHEN ASSIGNING THE ROLES.

> WHEN _____ (SITUATION) I NOTICED _____ (BEHAVIOR OF FRIEND).
> I FELT _____ (HOW THE BEHAVIOR MADE YOU OR OTHERS FEEL).
> HOW ABOUT _____ (SUGGESTION)?

AN APOLOGY can help you and a friend get through a fight or hurt feelings. Sometimes your friend will be the one apologizing. Sometimes you will be.

What makes an apology a heartfelt apology? It's not *just* about the words "I'm sorry."

Here are some tips to help you craft a genuine apology:

- ACKNOWLEDGE THAT SOMETHING YOU DID OR SAID WAS HURTFUL.
- EXPRESS REMORSE. IF YOU REGRET WHAT YOU SAID OR DID, SAY THAT.
- OFFER TO MAKE AMENDS BY MAKING UP FOR THE ACTION OR PROMISING IT WON'T HAPPEN AGAIN IN THE FUTURE.

For example:

> I'M SORRY THAT I BROKE YOUR NECKLACE WHEN I BORROWED IT. IT WAS AN ACCIDENT, BUT I KNOW I SHOULD BE MORE CAREFUL WITH BORROWED THINGS, AND I WILL BE FROM NOW ON. CAN I HELP YOU MAKE A NEW NECKLACE?

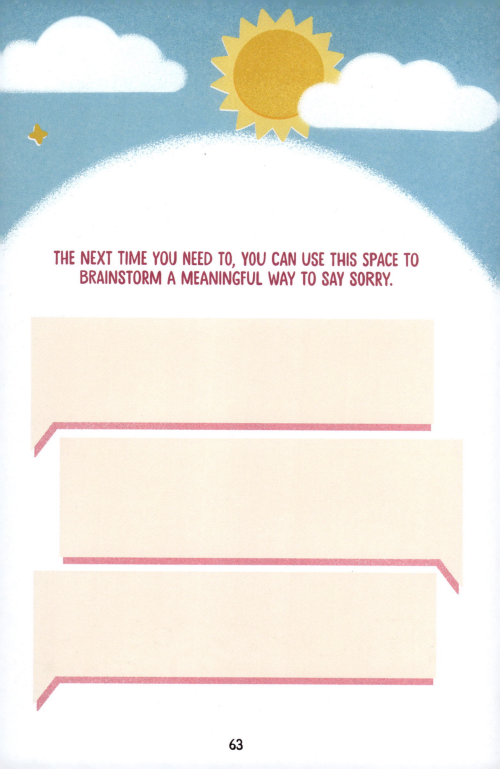

THE NEXT TIME YOU NEED TO, YOU CAN USE THIS SPACE TO BRAINSTORM A MEANINGFUL WAY TO SAY SORRY.

IF THINGS FEEL A LITTLE AWKWARD with a friend after a fight and an apology, try to remember why you're friends in the first place. What do you like about each other? What are activities you both like to do? Make a list and do one (or more) to get over the post-fight awkwardness.

FUN STUFF TO DO

THERE MAY COME A TIME when you need a break from a friend. Maybe you're growing apart and don't have the same interests anymore. Maybe they haven't been treating you nicely, and talking to them about it hasn't helped.

It's OK if you don't enjoy someone's company anymore. It's not OK to be mean or make fun of them as a way to initiate a break. Instead, try spending time with other friends and see how the break goes from there. It's OK to spend less time with one friend and more time with others, but it's not OK to cut off a friend with no explanation.

IF YOU THINK IT'S TIME FOR A BREAK FROM ONE OR MORE OF YOUR FRIENDSHIPS, CONSIDER THE FOLLOWING:

- ♥ WHAT DO YOU WANT TO GET OUT OF THIS BREAK? (FOR EXAMPLE, TIME WITH OTHER FRIENDS, A CHANCE TO THINK ABOUT THE FRIENDSHIP ON YOUR OWN, ETC.)
- ♥ WHAT WOULD YOU LIKE THIS FRIENDSHIP TO BE LIKE GOING FORWARD? (FOR EXAMPLE, MAYBE YOU SEE EACH OTHER ONLY AT SOCCER PRACTICE BUT DON'T NEED TO MESSAGE EVERY NIGHT, OR YOU STAY FRIENDS BUT STOP GOSSIPING OR TALKING ABOUT OTHER PEOPLE SO MUCH.)

TIP: If you don't like something your friend is doing and you don't think you can stay friends with them if they keep it up, you probably have to talk to them about it. (Flip to the previous pages for some help with that!)

TIP: If you just want a lower dose of your friend, maybe you don't need a big conversation but can pull back or respond less until the balance feels right to you.

SOMETIMES FRIENDSHIPS DON'T COME BACK FROM AN ARGUMENT.

HAVE YOU EVER CLOSED THE DOOR ON A FRIENDSHIP BECAUSE OF A FIGHT?

WHAT WAS THE FIGHT ABOUT?

WHAT ARE SOME FRIENDSHIP DEAL-BREAKERS (THINGS THAT MAKE YOU WANT TO END A FRIENDSHIP)?

WHAT ARE SOME ISSUES YOU THINK YOU *CAN* WORK THROUGH WITH A FRIEND?

"True friends are never apart, maybe in distance but never in heart."
—Unknown

CHALLENGES IN FRIENDSHIP aren't always about fighting. Do you have a friend who lives far away? Distance can make it hard to keep a friendship strong.

How can you stay close to a long-distance friend?

Real-life visits might not always be possible. Brainstorm all the fun ways you can keep in touch—you can even keep a list right here! Here are a few examples to get you started.

- Send one handwritten letter to each other per month. Getting mail is exciting, and writing a letter by hand makes it feel more personal.

- Schedule video calls every week or every month. If sitting and talking through a screen feels intimidating, try doing a shared activity while on the call—like doing your homework, cooking something delicious, or drawing.

- Share the things going on in your life with your friend and vice versa to see what your daily lives have in common, even when you're far apart. Keep a list right here!

-

-

-

-

-

HAVE YOU EVER been part of a friendship triangle or a clique with a few friends?

Friendship triangles and cliques can be tough because it can lead to some people feeling excluded by the others. Maybe you've felt excluded by friends before, or maybe someone else has felt excluded by you and another friend. Either way, it doesn't feel nice!

HOW DOES IT FEEL TO BE *INSIDE* A FRIEND GROUP?

HOW DOES IT FEEL TO BE *OUTSIDE* ONE?

REMEMBER: it's OK if you feel closer to one friend than another, and a friend having another close friend doesn't mean your own friendship is bad or less than. But if someone—you or another person—feels excluded, think about how to make that better.

HOW CAN YOU MAKE AN EFFORT TO INCLUDE SOMEONE WHO FEELS EXCLUDED, EVEN IF YOU AREN'T AS CLOSE TO THEM AS YOU ARE TO ANOTHER FRIEND?

Example: organize a group activity like going to the park after school, and make sure they can join in.

IF YOU FEEL EXCLUDED BY FRIENDS, HOW CAN YOU LET THEM KNOW?

TIP: flip back to page 59 to read about using "I" statements and letting friends know how you feel.

HOW CAN YOU BE PROACTIVE ABOUT FEELING MORE INCLUDED?

Example: take action and invite your friends over to your home for a group hang.

HOW DO YOU BALANCE different friends from different parts of your life? Maybe they don't know each other. Maybe they don't like each other. You might feel like you're stuck in the middle, always trying to balance friends or friend groups. No one likes to feel that way.

If your friends don't know each other, try introducing them. You might just end up with one big friend group, and that could lead to lots of fun.

BRAINSTORM SOME THINGS YOUR FRIENDS HAVE IN COMMON (HERE'S ONE: THEY BOTH LIKE *YOU*!).

_____

_____

_____

_____

_____

_____

_____

_____

_____

_____

_____

_____

NOW BRAINSTORM SOME CONVERSATION STARTERS TO BRING THEM TOGETHER.

HERE'S AN EXAMPLE:

Hi

HI, _____!
(FRIEND NAME)

I REALLY WANT TO HAVE YOU AND

MY OTHER FRIEND _____ OVER TO
(FRIEND NAME)

HANG OUT ALL TOGETHER. YOU BOTH REALLY LIKE

_____ AND I THINK YOU'LL GET
(THING IN COMMON)

ALONG. WHAT DO YOU THINK?

If your friends don't get along, think about why not. Is there a way to bring them together? If not, that's OK too—sometimes people just don't get along! Don't try to force your friends to be friends.

THINK ABOUT how your different friendships could actually be part of a bigger friendship web. Fill in the names of friends on the lines below to visualize those friendships turning into a web. You can even make the web bigger if you'd like!

Whenever you're feeling excluded or down for any reason, turn back to this friendship web to remember how many people you have in your life to go to for support.

THE NEXT TIME you're upset with a friend, try writing them a letter before talking about it. That way you can get all your feelings out in writing before hashing them out in person. You never have to deliver the letter if you don't want to—in fact, in most situations, you probably shouldn't deliver the letter, ever. But it can help you feel better to get your thoughts and feelings out on paper before having a conversation with a friend if you need to.

DRAFT YOUR LETTER HERE:

COMPROMISE is important when it comes to friendship. You want to stay true to yourself but also respect your friend (and your friendship).

Can you practice finding compromise using these overlapping circles?

FILL IN DISAGREEMENT TOPICS ON EACH SIDE (SEE EXAMPLE) AND USE THE MIDDLE SPACE TO COME UP WITH A POTENTIAL COMPROMISE:

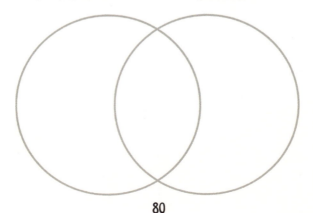

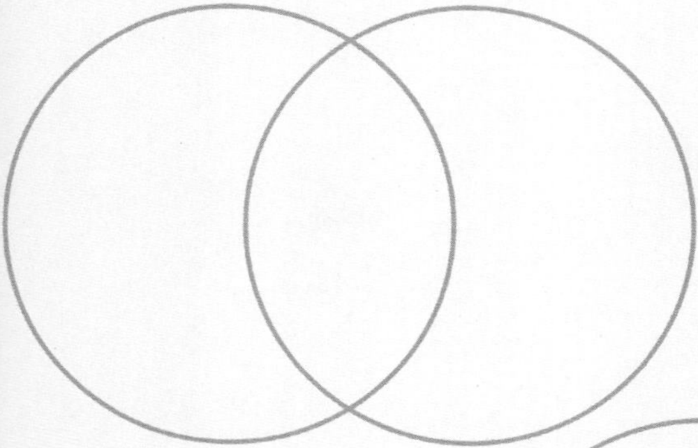

DISAGREEMENT TOPIC:

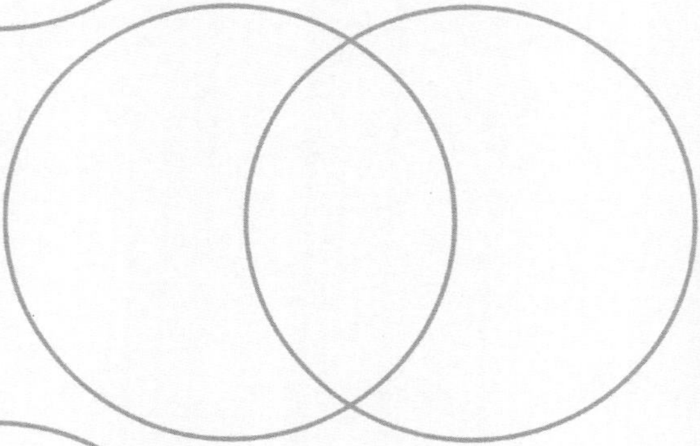

_____

_____

DISAGREEMENT TOPIC:

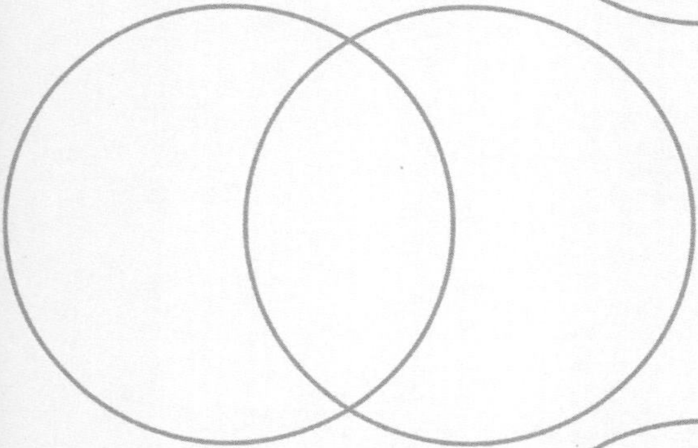

_____

_____

DISAGREEMENT TOPIC:

_____

_____

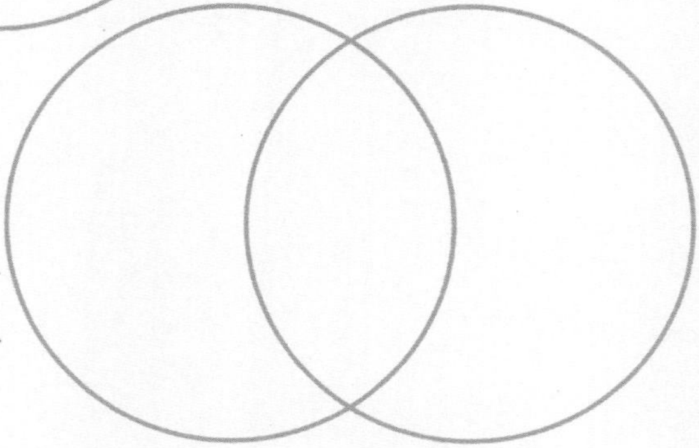

DISAGREEMENT TOPIC:

_____

_____

FRIENDSHIP CONFLICT feels bad in the moment, but it doesn't always mean bad things for your friendship. Conflict can actually be *good* for your friendship.

You can learn a lot about yourself and your friend because of a conflict.

Think about the Japanese art of kintsugi. Kintsugi refers to repairing broken items with gold. If you had a cracked teapot, for example, you would fill the cracks with gold to make the pot whole again, and it becomes even stronger and more beautiful than before.

Think about one of your friendships and a conflict you've had in that friendship. Write the conflict that caused the crack in that friendship in a crack on the teapot, then color over it in gold.

Then, in each gold section of the teapot, write something that improved about the friendship after the conflict.

This teapot is a reminder to yourself that you can come out stronger on the other side of an argument with a friend.

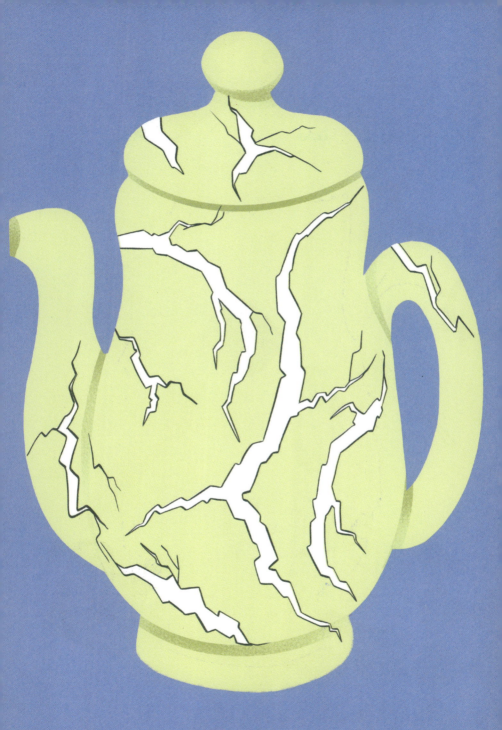

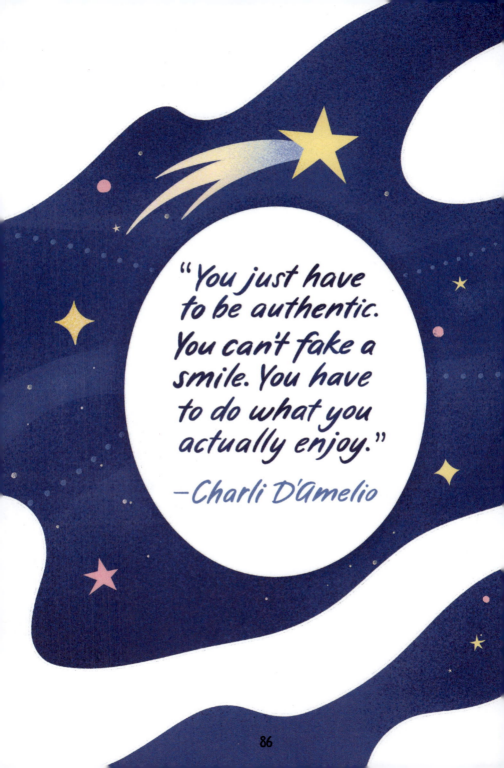

BEING YOURSELF

in any friendship is just as important as being a good friend. That could mean . . .

♥ STAYING TRUE TO WHO YOU ARE AND YOUR VALUES, EVEN WHEN FACING PRESSURE TO CHANGE;

♥ SPLITTING YOUR TIME WITH FRIENDS WITH ALONE TIME, FAMILY TIME, OR RESPONSIBILITIES;

♥ NOT PRETENDING TO LIKE CERTAIN THINGS TO IMPRESS A FRIEND;

♥ BALANCING YOUR INTERESTS WITH A FRIEND'S INTERESTS;

♥ AND MORE. . . .

How can you be your individual self even when you're part of a friend duo, trio, or big group?

SOMETIMES FRIENDS care about all the same things. Sometimes they don't. Both are OK! Just like you want to be accepted and supported as *your* individual self by your friends, it's important to accept and support friends for who they are and as they are.

CIRCLE THE THINGS ON THE LIST BELOW THAT ARE MOST IMPORTANT TO YOU:

Spending time with friends

Getting good grades

Spending time with family

Your hobby

Learning a new skill

Spending quiet time alone

Winning

Helping other people

Being nice

Making people laugh

Shopping

Helping animals

Earning money

Being organized

Spending time in nature

Being the center of attention

WRITE IN ANYTHING THAT'S MISSING FROM THE LIST ABOVE:

THEN ASK YOUR FRIEND WHICH OF THESE THINGS ARE IMPORTANT TO THEM AND CIRCLE THEIR ANSWERS HERE:

Spending time with friends
Getting good grades
Spending time with family
Your hobby
Learning a new skill
Spending quiet time alone
Winning
Helping other people
Being nice
Making people laugh
Shopping
Helping animals
Earning money
Being organized
Spending time in nature
Being the center of attention

WRITE IN ANYTHING THAT'S MISSING FROM THE LIST ABOVE:

LIST ALL THE THINGS THAT OVERLAP HERE. HOW CAN YOU TURN THESE THINGS INTO "TOGETHER TIME"?

A GREAT WAY to spend together time is to do something outside. Friendship is good for the body, mind, and soul, and so is spending time in the fresh air outdoors. What are some fun things you and your friend(s) can do together outside?

BRAINSTORM HERE:

_____

_____

_____

_____

_____

_____

_____

ONE *REALLY* FUN OUTDOOR ACTIVITY IS TIE-DYE.

Want to try it? Most tie-dye kits come with instructions, but here are a few extra tips just for you:

♥ FOR A COOL WATERCOLOR EFFECT, PILE ICE CUBES ON TOP OF YOUR FABRIC OF CHOICE. THEN SPRINKLE POWDERED DYE OVER THE ICE CUBES. WHEN THE ICE MELTS, THE POWDERED DYE MIXES WITH THE ICE WATER TO DYE YOUR T-SHIRT (OR WHATEVER PIECE OF FABRIC YOU'RE TIE-DYEING).

♥ YOU CAN REVERSE TIE-DYE BY USING BLEACH ON A DARK PIECE OF CLOTHING. AS WITH ALL TIE-DYEING, MAKE SURE TO ASK AN ADULT FOR HELP GETTING SET UP AND USING THE DYE/BLEACH SAFELY, AND WEAR DISPOSABLE GLOVES.

♥ COTTON FABRIC IS A GREAT CHOICE FOR TIE-DYEING. OTHER FABRICS, LIKE SPANDEX, POLYESTER, AND NYLON, WON'T HOLD THE DYE VERY WELL.

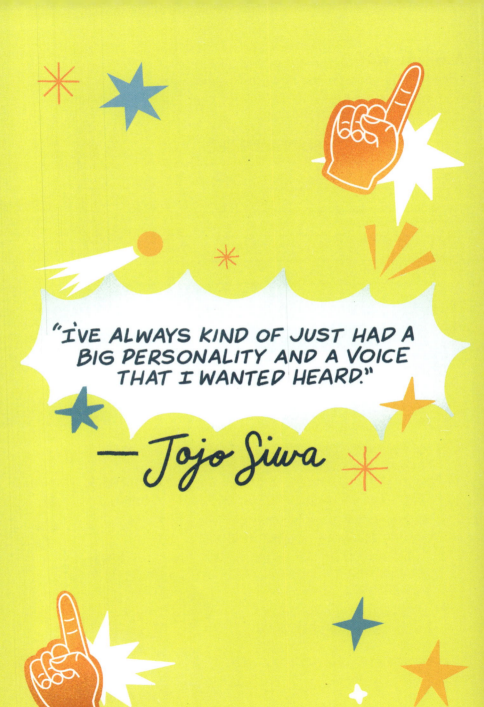

YOU MAY HAVE GOALS that are different than your BFF's. Maybe you want to join the basketball team next year and they want to star in the school play. Or they want to be president one day, and you want to be a librarian.

And it can be easy to get really into a friendship and forget to pay attention to your goals for a while. So, take a moment to brainstorm how your friendship can support *both* of your goals.

#GOALS

HOW CAN YOUR FRIENDS SUPPORT YOU IN YOUR GOALS?

HOW CAN YOU SUPPORT YOUR FRIENDS IN THEIR GOALS?

HOW CAN YOU MAKE SURE YOU STAY FOCUSED ON YOUR OWN GOALS? LIST YOUR TOP THREE GOALS AND AT LEAST ONE WAY YOU'LL WORK TOWARD THEM THIS YEAR:

SHARING INTERESTS can be an important foundation for friendship, but you and your friend(s) won't share *every* interest you have—that would probably get boring after a while.

USE THE SPACE BELOW TO FILL IN THE INTERESTS YOU HAVE ON THE LEFT, THE INTERESTS YOUR FRIEND HAS ON THE RIGHT, AND THE INTERESTS YOU SHARE IN THE MIDDLE, WHERE THE CIRCLES OVERLAP.

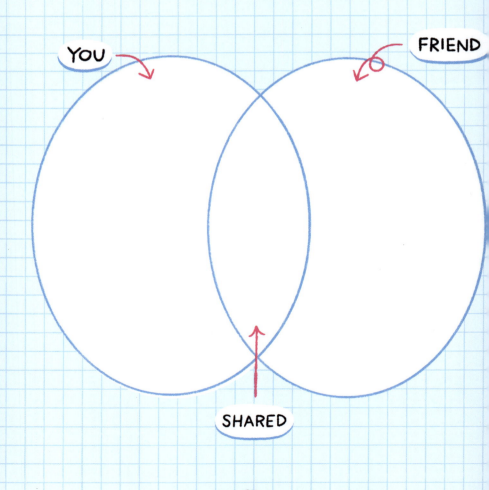

TAKE A MOMENT TO REFLECT: WHAT ARE SOME THINGS YOU CAN DO TOGETHER THAT YOU'LL BOTH ENJOY, BASED ON THE SHARED INTERESTS YOU LISTED?

HOW DO YOUR DIFFERENT INTERESTS ADD TO YOUR FRIENDSHIP?

HOW ARE THE THINGS YOU DO JUST FOR YOU DIFFERENT FROM WHAT YOU LIKE TO DO WITH FRIENDS?

DURING A REGULAR SCHOOL WEEK,

how are you spending your time? Make the empty circle below into a pie chart by coloring in the circle in sections that represent how you spend your time.

HERE'S AN EXAMPLE

Your turn!

- ☐ Time with Friends
- ☐ Family Time
- ☐ Me Time 🙂
- ☐ School
- ☐ Homework ✏️
- ☐ After-School Activities
- ☐ Other

LOOKING AT YOUR PIE CHART, DO YOU WISH YOU HAD SPENT YOUR TIME DIFFERENTLY? CIRCLE YOUR ANSWER.

YES   NO   MAYBE

IS THERE ANYTHING YOU CAN DO TO CHANGE HOW YOU SPEND YOUR TIME SO YOU HAVE MORE TIME FOR THE THINGS THAT ARE MOST IMPORTANT TO YOU?

_____
_____
_____
_____
_____
_____
_____
_____
_____
_____
_____
_____
_____
_____
_____
_____
_____
_____

IT'S SLEEPOVER TIME!

What would be the schedule for your perfect sleepover party?

FILL IT IN HERE:

hourly schedule

YAAAY! SLEEPOVER!!

: PM

: PM

: PM

: PM

: PM

: PM

P.S. If you're feeling nervous before a sleepover away from home with friends, that's totally normal. It might help to talk to a trusted adult about your nerves beforehand. Maybe even make a plan with them in case you decide you want to come home early.

SEEING YOURSELF through someone else's eyes—especially someone who loves you—can teach you a lot about yourself. It can give you a boost of confidence, too.

DRAW A PORTRAIT OF YOUR BESTIE HERE THAT INCLUDES ILLUSTRATIONS OF YOUR THREE FAVORITE THINGS ABOUT THEM.

FOR EXAMPLE, IF THEY MAKE REALLY GOOD FRENCH TOAST WHENEVER YOU HAVE SLEEPOVERS, YOU COULD DRAW THEM WEARING A CHEF'S HAT OR HOLDING A BOTTLE OF SYRUP.

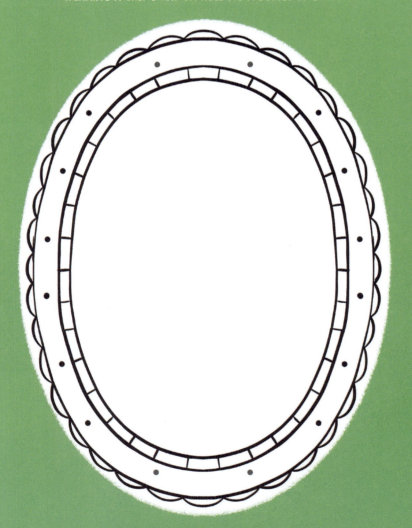

THEN ASK THEM TO DRAW A PORTRAIT OF YOU, WITH THEIR THREE FAVORITE
THINGS ABOUT YOU REPRESENTED, AND TAPE THE PORTRAIT HERE:

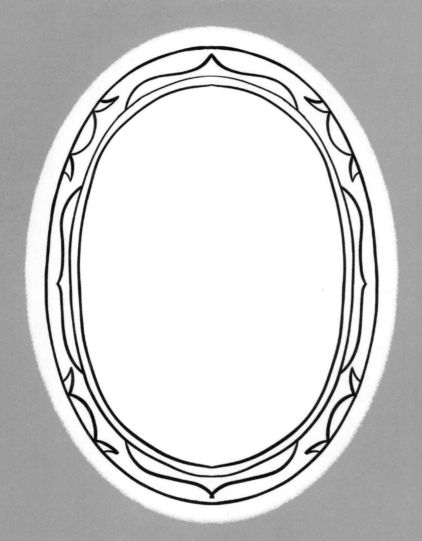

DOES THE WAY YOUR FRIEND DREW YOU MATCH UP WITH HOW YOU
SEE YOURSELF? DID ANYTHING IN THE PORTRAIT SURPRISE YOU?

ASK YOUR FRIEND MORE QUESTIONS

to keep the conversation going! Use the questions below to get to know your friend even better than you already do.

What's your favorite subject in school and why? What do you think mine is?

_____

What's one thing we each really like about each other?

_____

If we each had to describe each other with one word, that word would be:

_____

If we each had to describe our friendship with one word, that word would be:

_____

One thing we each want to do together sometime soon is:

_____

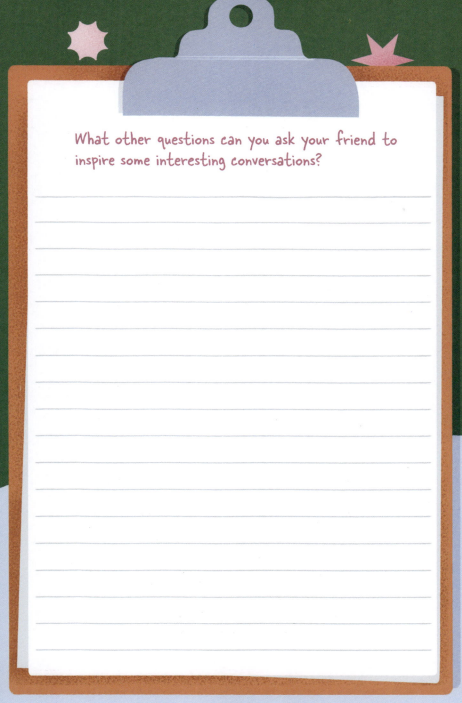

What other questions can you ask your friend to inspire some interesting conversations?

THE FUN OF FRIENDSHIP

isn't just about making friends, being a good friend, and getting through the tough times together—you've also got to celebrate and cherish those friendships.

But how?

- ♥ HOW CAN YOU CELEBRATE YOUR FRIENDS AND MAKE SURE YOU FEEL CELEBRATED IN RETURN?
- ♥ WHAT ARE SOME FUN THINGS YOU AND YOUR BFFS CAN DO TOGETHER?
- ♥ HOW CAN YOU KEEP THOSE BONDS OF FRIENDSHIP STRONG?

In this section, you'll find ideas and activities for all the above and more.

HAVE YOU EVER USED ABSTRACT ART TO EXPRESS HOW YOU FEEL?

Well, let's give it a try.

Think about one of your friendships and use this space to draw how you feel about that friendship.

Be as abstract as you want—you could even just scribble all over the page. Think about your color choices, too: for example, using blue could signify that you feel a sense of calm when you think about this friendship. A lot of red could mean that you feel angry toward this friend. But what the colors mean are up to you!

ONE WAY TO CELEBRATE YOUR FRIENDS is to think about why you appreciate them. What about them makes you feel grateful for their friendship?

USE THE SPACES BELOW TO MAKE A LIST OF YOUR FRIENDS AND ONE THING YOU APPRECIATE ABOUT EACH FRIENDSHIP.

NAME: _____

ONE THING I APPRECIATE ABOUT OUR FRIENDSHIP IS . . .
_____
_____

NAME: _____

ONE THING I APPRECIATE ABOUT OUR FRIENDSHIP IS . . .
_____
_____

NAME: _____

ONE THING I APPRECIATE ABOUT OUR FRIENDSHIP IS . . .

_____
_____

NAME: _____

ONE THING I APPRECIATE

ABOUT OUR FRIENDSHIP

IS . . .

_____
_____
_____

NAME: _____

ONE THING I APPRECIATE

ABOUT OUR FRIENDSHIP

IS . . .

_____
_____
_____

NAME: _____

ONE THING I APPRECIATE ABOUT OUR FRIENDSHIP IS . . .

_____
_____

IN A BRAIDED ROPE, different pieces come together, intertwining to make something beautiful and strong.

Think about your friend group like a braided rope for a moment—what are each of your friends bringing to the group to make it beautiful and strong?

LIST THOSE THINGS HERE:

And braided ropes get even stronger when you tie them into a knot.

DO YOU KNOW HOW TO TIE A FRIENDSHIP KNOT? (YES, THAT'S A REAL NAME OF A TYPE OF KNOT!) GRAB SOME STRING, ROPE, OR SHOELACES AND GIVE IT A TRY!

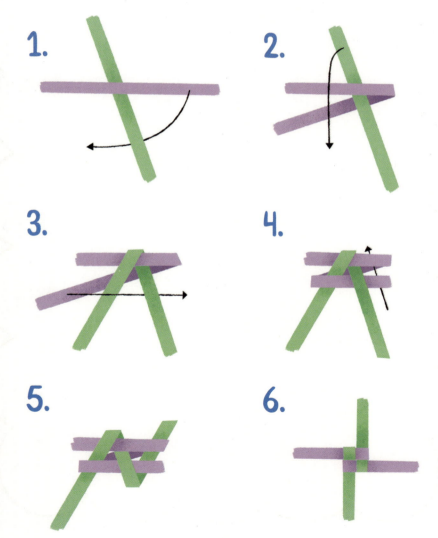

DO YOU HAVE FRIENDSHIP MEMORIES THAT MAKE YOU SMILE WHEN YOU THINK ABOUT THEM?

WRITE ABOUT ONE OF YOUR FAVORITE MEMORIES WITH YOUR FRIEND(S) HERE:

IF YOU AND YOUR FRIEND WERE THE MAIN CHARACTERS IN A BOOK ABOUT YOUR FRIENDSHIP, WHAT WOULD THE BOOK COVER LOOK LIKE? ILLUSTRATE IT HERE:

SOMETIMES it's easier to express your feelings with a song . . . or a whole playlist. Use this space to brainstorm a playlist full of songs that remind you of your friends.

The next time you all hang out, you can surprise them by playing it and enjoying the music together. Maybe you'll even feel inspired to make up a dance to one of the songs.

TIME TO PUT YOUR IMAGINATION TO WORK:

What's a fantasy vacation you and your BFF hope to take together one day? Imagine it here:

DO YOU EVER FEEL like the friendship between you and your friend was written in the stars? Like you were meant to be friends? That's a pretty special feeling.

If you and your friend were a constellation in the night sky, what would it look like?

USE STARS TO FORM THE SHAPE OF IT HERE:

SURPRISES CAN BE SMALL,

like finding an extra piece of gum in your backpack. Or they can be big, like when your favorite cousin shows up for an unplanned visit. Either way, surprises keep things interesting.

To celebrate your friend(s), plan a surprise for them—big or small. Think back to earlier in this book when you thought about how different people like to be/feel appreciated, and use that info here—you want to make sure you're expressing your appreciation for your friend in a way that they're comfortable with.

USE THIS SPACE TO BRAINSTORM AND PLAN. HERE ARE SOME IDEAS TO GET YOU STARTED:

- Decorate their locker on a random day, just because.
- Throw a surprise party on their half birthday. They'll never expect it.
-
-
-
-
-
-
-
-
-
-

FRIENDSHIP IS A TWO-WAY STREET, which means you should feel as celebrated by your friend(s) as you make them feel.

DO YOU FEEL LIKE YOUR FRIEND(S) CELEBRATE YOUR FRIENDSHIP? HOW?

_____
_____
_____
_____
_____
_____
_____
_____

AND IF THEY COULD DO BETTER, HOW WOULD YOU WANT TO BE CELEBRATED?

_____
_____
_____
_____
_____
_____
_____
_____

YOU AND YOUR FRIENDS ARE SPECIAL, that's obvious. But what makes each of your friends special?

WHICH ONE OF YOUR FRIENDS IS MOST LIKELY TO:

- ♥ GET STRAIGHT A'S: _____
- ♥ HAVE PAINT SPLATTERED ON THEIR CLOTHES: _____
- ♥ SAVE THEIR ALLOWANCE TO BUY SOMETHING SPECIAL: _____
- ♥ PLAY A DIFFERENT SPORT EVERY SEASON: _____
- ♥ GIVE YOU A TISSUE WHEN YOU'RE SAD: _____
- ♥ PASS YOU A NOTE IN CLASS: _____

WHAT ARE SOME OTHER "MOST LIKELY TO" AWARDS YOU'D LIKE TO GIVE TO YOUR FRIENDS?

IT CAN FEEL GOOD to receive a compliment. It can feel even better to *give* one. How can you go beyond the surface and let a friend know what you like most about them?

USE THE WORDS AND PHRASES BELOW TO CRAFT A FEW REALLY SPECIAL COMPLIMENTS TO GIVE TO YOUR FRIENDS THE NEXT TIME YOU SEE THEM.

THOUGHTFUL
CLEVER
GENEROUS
ENTHUSIASTIC
FULL OF GOOD ADVICE
CREATIVE
FUNNY
TALENTED
ARTISTIC
HELPFUL
A GREAT LISTENER
JOYFUL
OPTIMISTIC

HERE ARE SOME EXAMPLES:

You are so funny. When you _____ I laughed so hard I cried.

I think it's cool how creative you are. It was so awesome how you _____.

Write your own here:

"Find a group of people who challenge and inspire you; spend a lot of time with them, and it will change your life."
— Amy Poehler

WHEN YOU RECEIVE A COMPLIMENT FROM A FRIEND THAT MEANS A LOT TO YOU, WRITE IT DOWN HERE. THAT WAY, WHENEVER YOU'RE FEELING BLUE, YOU CAN FLIP BACK TO THIS PAGE AND REMEMBER HOW MUCH YOUR FRIENDS LOVE, ADMIRE, OR CELEBRATE *YOU*!

IT'S TIME TO CHANNEL YOUR INNER POET.
YOU'LL HAVE A POEM BEFORE YOU KNOW IT.
USE EACH LETTER BELOW TO WRITE SOME LINES,
THINKING ABOUT YOUR BEST-OF-FRIEND TIMES.

(This is an acrostic poem, which is when the first letter of each line spells out a word, in this case, FRIENDSHIP.)

f _____

r _____

i _____

e _____

n _____

d _____

s _____

h _____

i _____

p _____

NOW WRITE ANOTHER ACROSTIC POEM USING ONE OF YOUR FRIENDS' NAMES:

IT'S FUN TO THINK ABOUT THE FUTURE—especially when you're imagining you and your friends in it.

Use a square piece of paper to make a fortune teller and write some futuristic fortunes inside—some silly, some serious, all with a friendship theme.

Then play with your friends to predict their (and your) futures.

Use this space to brainstorm fortunes:

Here are some examples:

- THE NEXT PERSON YOU SEE WEARING YOUR FAVORITE COLOR IS DESTINED TO BE YOUR BFF.
- THE NEXT TIME YOU NEED HELP, ASK A FRIEND. TOGETHER, YOU CAN GO FAR.
- KEEP YOUR FRIENDS CLOSE. YOUR CONNECTIONS WILL HELP YOU ALL SHINE BRIGHTEST.
- THERE WILL BE AN ICE CREAM SUNDAE IN YOUR HAND SOON. SHARE IT WITH A BUDDY TO EAT IT BEFORE IT MELTS!

_____
_____
_____
_____
_____
_____
_____
_____

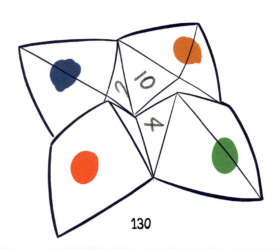

HOW TO MAKE A FORTUNE TELLER

 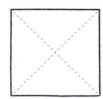

Fold the paper in half diagonally, unfold, then repeat the other way.

 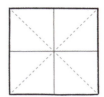

Fold the paper in half, unfold, then repeat the other way.

 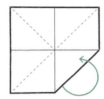

Fold the corners into the center, forming a smaller square.

 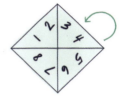

Flip the smaller square over and fold the corners into the center, forming an even smaller square. Write numbers on each triangle.

Open the flaps and write fortunes underneath each.

Close the flaps and flip the square over. Write a color on each square.

Fold in half.

Slide your fingers underneath the squares to work the fortune teller.

NOW LET'S *PICTURE* THE FUTURE. Use this page to draw you and a friend ten years from now.

What will be the same about your friendship? What will be different? What will you do together for fun?

STAY IN THE FUTURE FOR A SEC. Write a note to your BFF to share with them in five years. What do you hope your friendship will be like then? What do you hope the two of you would've done together by then?

DATE: _____

NOW, ASK YOUR FRIEND to write a note to future you. Fold it up and tape it here—make sure not to read it until five years from now.

DATE: _____

SOMETIMES, like if a friend is in an unsafe situation or at risk of harm from themselves or others, it's important to ask for help, even if a friend has confided in you and expects the secret to stay a secret. Your friend might be upset later, but it's more important to keep your friend safe. That's what good friends do. You can ask for help from an adult you trust (like an adult from the list you made on page 41), and there are additional resources you can turn to as well. Here are some free resources that can help:

NATIONAL ALLIANCE ON MENTAL ILLNESS: NAMI.ORG

NATIONAL ALLIANCE FOR EATING DISORDERS: ALLIANCEFOREATINGDISORDERS.COM

HOTLINES:
- ♥ **SUICIDE & CRISIS LIFELINE: CALL 988 OR VISIT 988LIFELINE.ORG**
- ♥ **CRISIS TEXT LINE: TEXT "HOME" TO 741741 OR CHAT ONLINE AT CRISISTEXTLINE.ORG**
- ♥ **CHILDHELP NATIONAL CHILD ABUSE HOTLINE: CALL OR TEXT 800-422-4453 OR CHAT ONLINE AT CHILDHELPHOTLINE.ORG**